DENETSOSIE

Written by
Broderick H. Johnson, Editor
Sydney M. Callaway
and Others

Illustrated by
Andy Tsinajinnie

NAVAJO CURRICULUM CENTER PRESS
2218 EAST MAGNOLIA
PHOENIX, ARIZONA 85034

1974

International Standard Book Number: 0-89019-007-0
Library of Congress Catalog Card Number: 73-93973

Manufactured in the United States of America

**O'SULLIVAN
WOODSIDE
& COMPANY**
2218 East Magnolia
Phoenix, Arizona 85034

To the members of Denetsosie's family, who revere his memory and who have done much to make the book possible, this volume is dedicated.

A Talk with Navajo Students

by John Dick
Member, Board of Education
Rough Rock Demonstration School

I SHOULD LIKE TO SAY a few words concerning Denetsosie who was a leader and medicine man among the Navajo people. When he was a young man he went to school as much as was possible for him in those days, and he learned all he could. In addition, he learned a great deal about the sings and other ceremonies of the Navajos. Because of his knowledge and character, relatives and friends and those who came in contact with him over the years gained much knowledge about the background and importance of the sings and ceremonies.

This book is the biography of Denetsosie, and, from reading it, the Navajo children of today and tomorrow also can learn more about the history and culture of their people. The story is largely an autobiography, as Denetsosie told it in the Navajo language. He has passed on to us many things that he learned as a young man and as a leader among his people. And those who knew him learned from him. As our children read of his life, they, too, can learn those important facts to make their lives stronger.

Denetsosie worked with sheep and cattle and in trade, as our people have done for many years. As you read of his experiences, you will learn more about our people and their way of life. You will understand them. And you will understand Denetsosie's thoughts about this changing world and about the future.

This man also served as a tribal councilman and as a chapter officer. His leadership was as great as his desire to help his people. From the time Denetsosie was old enough to be of service he gave continuously of his time and his knowledge to help others. I hope that as you read of these qualities you will be inspired to become leaders and to help your people as he did. It is men and women like him that we need among our people today.

Navajo students now and in the future must be able to learn about Denetsosie and other men with similar abilities if they are to become as great as he was. This and other good books have been written. Others will follow. If we will read these books and study them, we will be able to learn, but if we turn away from the things written about, we will lose the strength and power of our heritage.

It is important for us to remember who we are and that we are a strong and happy people. As we learn of, and remember, our great forefathers such as Denetsosie, we will be able to face the future of change with confidence and a sense of security.

DENETSOSIE

(Diné Ts'ósí)

THE GRANDMOTHER

A young girl who was to become Denetsosie's grandmother was one of many Navajos (Diné) who were kidnaped and sold into bondage during the early history of the American Southwest. She was about 14 years old.

Such captures, usually causing much heartbreak and suffering, had been common occurrences among the Navajos for many generations. In fact, stealing people and selling them had been a practice throughout the history of man. One tribe or group would raid another, kill or chase away some of the men and carry off the women, children and other men as slaves.

In the southwestern part of what is now the United States, such kidnaping had become a way of life for the various Indian tribes, as well as for the Spaniards and, later, the Mexicans. This had been going on for many scores of years before the United States took possession of the land and governed its people, beginning in 1848 with the treaty of Guadalupe Hidalgo.

Raids and counter-raids were almost constant. Fear and turmoil were everywhere. For the Navajos it was the Utes (Nóóda'á), Apaches (Dził ghą́'ą́) and Comanches (Anaałání) with whom they had to contend — or it was the Mexicans (Naakai).

1

After traveling all night in a severe snowstorm, the group of Navajos, cold and weary, rested and killed sheep to roast. Among them was Naakai 'Asdzą́ą́ who became Denetsosie's grandmother.

In those early days Navajo families traveled around a lot, looking for new locations that would give better protection from the weather, as well as from raiders, and, at the same time, would offer good hunting and adequate grazing for their livestock.

Denetsosie's ancestors, for example, had moved about in a large region from Tódzis'a (lower Wheatfields area) to Dziłíjiin (Black Mountain), beyond it to T'áásahdii dah 'azkání (Separate Square Rock) down to Tséyi' (Chinle) and back to Wheatfields. No one ever said, "This is **my** land, this is where I live." They had no wagons. They rode horses or walked, taking their sheep with them. Of course, there were not nearly as many Navajos at that

The girl and her mother, only a few yards away, watched their Navajo relatives being captured and their livestock rounded up by Mexican raiders.

time as there are now. Compared with today, there was plenty of room in which to move around.

One of the family groups that decided to move during a winter in the late 1850s was that of Denetsosie's grandmother, later known as Naakai 'Asdzą́ą́ (Mexican Lady). The members were leaving Béésh Nahałdaas (Falling Iron) at the north side of Sǫ' silá (Laid Out Like a Star — Sonsela Butte), which now is in Arizona but very close to New Mexico, in the Ch'óóshgai (Chuska) Mountains.

Because they knew that they were being followed by raiding Mexicans, they traveled all night during a wind and snow storm. At daybreak, tired and worn, they camped at a suitable place. They had to eat and rest. They killed sheep to roast and prepared other food. The

3

men went out to scout for the Mexicans. Only the women and children were left, and a couple of elderly men.

Naakai 'Asdzą́ą́ and her mother moved a short distance from the main camp to watch for the enemy. But they were sleepy, and they soon dozed. Suddenly they were awakened by loud noises. Somehow, the Mexicans had slipped past the Navajo scouts in the snow storm and had found the camp. The people were running about in great confusion, screaming and crying. Some of the raiders were rounding up the livestock. Others were capturing the women and children.

The girl and her mother were terribly frightened. They thought of hiding until the Mexicans had gone with their captives, but that would have left the two alone in a strange place. They had no food. They probably would have frozen to death. They thought of walking into the camp and joining the others as prisoners. But they did not have to decide. Several Mexicans saw them and grabbed them.

The captors and captives headed toward Tsoodził (Mount Taylor). Snow fell again that night and continued all the next day and night. They were forced to build a big fire to keep from freezing, and the captives were ordered to remove their moccasins to make it harder to escape. They tried to dry the moccasins and their clothes by the campfire.

The entire group was gathered around the fire when a band of Navajo warriors caught up with the raiding party.

During the fighting that followed a Navajo scout called to the captives to run away. But they were barefooted and closely guarded, and they could do nothing but hope for a better chance later. So the warriors left after they had re-taken some of their livestock. The next morning the captives noticed that many of the Mexicans had scratches

4

Navajo warriors recovered some of the animals, but the prisoners were not able to run away.

and bruises and that some were limping or badly hurt, showing that they had been wounded or run down by the Navajos' horses and that it had been a hard fight.

About noon that day the group reached the little village of Tł'oh chiní (Ramah), New Mexico, where Mexican women came running with whips made of reeds and began to lash the captive girls and women.

The group stayed at Ramah that day, and, early the next morning, started for Mexico. A Mexican with one white eye ("not very good looking," as Denetsosie said his grandmother described him) had captured Naakai 'Asdzáá, and the girl was afraid of him. From Ramah he had with him his father and mother, both of whom were old. They were very poor. They had scarcely any food — just tortillas and beans. They offered her food, but it looked spoiled; so she refused to eat. She preferred to starve. She said later that she had wanted to die.

They camped several times before getting to Mexico; and, two days later, a Mexican man from Be'aldííldahsinil

5

At Ramah, in New Mexico, the Mexican women lashed
the captive women and girls.

(Albuquerque) bargained for her. She recalled later that
he paid for her in Mexican silver pesos.

The man took her to Albuquerque and gave her to his
young son for a wife. She was made a member of the
household, where her life was not too bad. The man who
had bought her was a leader of the Mexicans. She was
treated kindly. Along with other members of the family,
she did household chores, and she took part in the family's
social life.

Denetsosie did not know how many years his grandmother lived in Albuquerque. While she was there,
Asdzą́ą́ɫ chíí' (Red Woman), who became Denetsosie's
mother, was born.

6

A Mexican leader bought Naakai 'Asdzą́ą́ from her captors and took her to Albuquerque.

A treaty had been signed in 1868 at Hwééldi (Fort Sumner), New Mexico, between the United States and the Navajos which guaranteed that the Navajos would be returned to their homeland after four years of miserable exile following the Long Walk. After gathering their meager possessions, the Navajos began to move slowly toward Tséhootso (Fort Defiance). Finally they came to the Rio Grande River, south of Albuquerque. Many Mexican settlers were watching the procession. After crossing the river, the Navajos made camp.

Some of the Navajos thought they recognized a Navajo woman among the Mexicans. And they were sure of who she was when one of the men who had known her as a child remembered that Naakai 'Asdzą́ą́ had a finger nail missing when she was captured. Her bosom seemed full,

7

as though she might be nursing a baby. That turned out to be true. The baby girl was brought.

At first Naakai 'Asdzą́ą́ did not want to leave her home in Albuquerque. She pretended that she did not understand Navajo. But she was persuaded to change her mind, and she decided to return to her native land. The woman truly was Naakai 'Asdząą́, and the little girl was Asdząą́ł chíí'.

The woman married again after her return to the Reservation. Her second husband was a medicine man. His name was Tséyi'nii Yázhí, or Tséyi'nii Ts'ósí. He was a singer of Flint Way (Béshee), Blessing Way (Hózhǫ́ǫ́jí) and the Lightning and Shooting Chant (Naat'oii).

BIRTH AND BOYHOOD OF DENETSOSIE

Asdząą́ł chíí' grew up near Lók'aa'ché'gai (Lukachukai). She married Hastiin Tábaahá (Edge of Water Man), who became Denetsosie's father. He and Asdząą́ł chíí' were on their way to Wheatfields, Arizona, from Kin naazíní (Standing Houses) when the boy was born in 1891.*

The marriage did not last long. One day Hastiin Tábaahá just left his wife and Denetsosie and the other children. After that, the family was very poor. Mother and children did not eat well. They had no coffee. They had no shoes. Clothing was scarce. The only pants the boys had were made of thin white cloth. Fortunately, Asdząą́ł chíí' married a policeman from Shash bitoo (Fort Wingate). His name was Tsii'agodí (Short Cut Hair). His clan was Tó'aheedlíinii (Where the Waters Come Together).

Denetsosie was only a little boy. He said recently, "At that time married couples sometimes did not live together very long. A woman never went after her husband

---

* According to his census card on file in Window Rock, the Navajo capital, Denetsosie stated on August 8, 1928, that he had been born in 1891.

8

The Navajo exiles at Fort Sumner long had dreamed of leaving the miserable place and returning to their beloved mountains, buttes and plateaus.

when he left because it was never said, 'So-and-so went after her husband.' Maybe it was because they did not care."

Tsii'agodí was a very busy man and seldom was at home. The Navajos were having trouble with the Chiricahua Apaches (Chíshí), and that "tied him down a lot," as Denetsosie explained.

Still, he went home to his new family as often as he could. He told the mother and children that they would build a hogan (hooghan) and prepare the land that was overgrown with sagebrush. He told them to settle down at Wheatfields and make it their home. He went with them into the forest to cut pine trees, and they brought the poles home on their shoulders or dragged them. Some

9

Denetsosie's mother, Asdzą́ą́ł chíí', worked very hard to provide food for her family.

small ones were pulled out with the roots and planted near the hogan. They had no wagon at that time. They had only one old horse.

Denetsosie commented, "We had to carry firewood wrapped in blankets on our backs. We did not have shoes. Our pants and shirts still were made of flour sacks and other bits of cloth that our mother found somewhere. But no one ever complained. We just wore what we could get."

The stepfather was kind and understanding, and he was a patient man. Soon, with all of them working together, the family began to live happily. He saw to it that they received their share of government supplies from Fort Defiance. They got a narrow plow with a "head" four inches wide. Denetsosie remembered, "We used our one horse to pull it. One of us led the horse and another was at the back guiding the plow."

10

The method worked. Later the family got another horse.

Also, over a period of time, and usually one item at a time, the family was given shovels, hoes, files, a pick, an ax and a hammer. Then, a wonderful gift from the white men in Fort Defiance was a wagon. And, finally, came a sickle to help harvest the wheat. Even with the new tools, the planting, cultivating and harvesting was very hard work, especially for the boys. Denetsosie commented, "All of us worked hard all of the time. And we could not have succeeded if it had not been for my mother. She was a strong woman. She used to grind wheat on stones to make tortillas (náneeskaadí). At first it was our only food. We did not have much to eat until after we harvested our first good crops."

Tsii'agodí taught the boys to hoe the weeds away from the wheat and corn and to irrigate when there was water.

Cutting the wheat — sometimes with a crude scythe, sometimes with a one-handed sickle — was slow and back-breaking work.

The fields of some of their neighbors were mostly weeds. They just let "sunflowers" grow with their crops. But Denetsosie's family had clean fields. He said later that they "seemed to hoe all the time." The boys were proud of what they were doing. They respected their stepfather who had given them a new chance. He made them feel that each of them was somebody. They stood up straight. They were not ashamed, no matter whom they were with.

In the fall they cut the wheat with their peculiar knife which was "shaped like an elbow" (the sickle). A person swung it in one hand and could cut only a small part of the field each day. They piled the wheat so that all of the stems were in one direction. Then they made a threshing floor of hard earth for harvesting the grain. First they selected a good flat spot, watered it, let it dry and then drove the sheep over it again and again to

To help thresh the wheat, the men sometimes rode their horses 'round and 'round over it, thus separating the grains from the husks and stalks.

The women and girls gleaned the fields of every possible head of wheat and threshed them over sheepskins.

trample it down and harden it. The wheat then was spread out on that spot and the sheep were driven over it many times. Sometimes boys and men would mount their horses and ride around and around over the piled wheat to separate the grains from the stalks. Other men kept turning the wheat, and they helped to separate the grains from the straw and husks by tossing the mixture into the air. It was a kind of game. In those days neighbors helped each other more than they do now, according to Denetsosie.

When the first threshing was completed, the men gathered the grain in goatskin bags or buckets. These were held high as the grain was poured out. It was done on windy days, and the breeze blew the chaff away, while the grain fell onto skins stretched below. The grain then was ready to be sacked and hauled home in the wagon.

Meanwhile, the girls and women were busy. They had gleaned the heads of wheat that the reapers had left in the stubblefields. They threshed those heads on sheepskins and carried the grain home to be ground. They did not want to lose any of it.

The method was similar to that used by reapers for many, many centuries in other parts of the world.

The corn was harvested just as carefully. Among the Navajos none of the crop was wasted. The older women remembered only too well how, at one time, even as late as after the return from Fort Sumner, they had had to use wild seeds for food.

For the first year or two Denetsosie's family did not have much wheat to harvest. Later, as he said, "they harvested a lot of both wheat and corn."

After the threshing, relatives of Tsii'agodí and Asdzą́ą́ł chíí' came from Black Mountain and other places to visit them and were given some of the harvest.

The women made the wheat into flour by hand. They used grinding stones because there was no grist mill in the area at that time.

Besides good crops of wheat and corn, Denetsosie's family also increased the number of horses and sheep that it owned.

SCHOOL DAYS
AND LEARNING TO BE A MEDICINE MAN

Denetsosie was about 12 years old when he was sent to school at Fort Defiance. He attended there for three years but he did not learn much. He explained, "I did not come to an understanding of the things I was supposed to learn about."

14

However, he worked in the boiler room of the power-house and did learn useful things there. Then he was transferred to the Albuquerque Indian School, where he stayed for three years. But he said that he did not learn much there, either, because he was too interested in sports. He was an excellent athlete and was on the number one teams in baseball, basketball and track. He also played football. Much of his time was spent traveling with the school teams, according to his account.

Hastiin Dághaał chíí' (Red Mustache Man), an older brother, was interested in the boy's education and was worried when he learned that Denetsosie was spending most of his time in athletic activities.

"What are you going to do to support yourself?" Hastiin Dághaał chíí' often asked.

Nevertheless, Denetsosie quit school and went to his mother's home. She wanted him to do it because she needed his help. He said, "Even though I was in school for six years, I finished only the third grade. We did not spend much time in classroom learning. We won many trophies in sports, and I helped win some of them."

Hastiin Dághaał chíí' was son-in-law to a medicine man, Hastiin Doo yáłti'í (Man Who Does Not Talk), and he had learned some of the songs of the Lightning and Shooting Way Ceremony (Naat'oii). Hastiin Doo yáłti'í asked Denetsosie to learn to sing, and the boy thought it over and decided that he wanted to learn. The medicine man had asked Denetsosie what he had learned in school, and the lad had answered, "Not very much. I had to have an interpreter to learn what I did."

"From now on I want you to go with me when I sing," Doo yáłti'í said. "You will learn very quickly that way." The old man had learned to sing from Hastiin Niteelí

(Wide Man), who was of the Tó'aheedlíiníí (Where Waters Meet) clan.

So Denetsosie began helping Doo yáłti'í. He did some of the sandpaintings (iikááh) and other work that was part of the ceremonies. At first he prepared the simpler sandpaintings. Later he learned the more difficult ones. He also learned how to do the Thunderbird and Sun sandpaintings. He said that some people want to learn to be medicine men in a year, but that it cannot be done. He insisted that many years are needed. Some men say, "I have learned everything." But Denetsosie said, "I started to learn as a boy, and, even though I observed and gained experience for many years, there always was something else to learn."

The young man lived with his brother for three years; then they went to Zhealy Tso's Trading Post, which was near T'iis yázhí łání (Valley Store) between Dá'ák'e halání (Many Farms) and Ch'ínlį́ (Chinle). Hastiin Dághaał chíí' became the storekeeper, and the owner asked Denetsosie to stay there, too. Denetsosie spent a year helping his brother while he learned more about becoming a medicine man.

Young Denetsosie learned to do sandpaintings, and he studied for many years to become a medicine man.

One day a Navajo man came into the trading post. Denetsosie noticed that the man kept looking at him. Finally, the man came over to the boy and spoke. He said that he was Hastiin Tábąąhá (Edge of Water Man), the lad's real father. It had been nearly 20 years since he had left his family at Wheatfields. Most young men would have resented their father doing what this man had done to his family. But Denetsosie was of a forgiving nature. He could not hate anyone, especially his real father, no matter what the man had done.

"I thought he had just forgotten me after all those years," Denetsosie commented later.

Soon afterward, his father came to the post again and said, "My son, there is a woman here who has horses and sheep. Her father and mother also have horses and sheep. This woman really can weave a rug, and she knows how to handle sheep, too. I have been to their place and have asked her parents if it is all right for you to marry their daughter. I asked her, too. They all agreed. I want you to marry her. She is of the Tódích'íí'nii clan.

MARRIAGE

Denetsosie was in no hurry to see the girl. He had become interested in learning to be a medicine man. Girls, at that time, were far from his thoughts. He told his father that he wanted to think about it. His father kept coming back and talking, however, and finally Denetsosie decided to find out what kind of a woman she was. There was to be a Nidáá' (Squaw Dance) at her place, and he decided to go.

All Navajo ceremonials have a time for fun and visiting. People come mainly for the religious benefits or to take part. But they also come to see and be seen, to talk and to listen. 'Anaa'jí (Enemy Way) is that kind of ceremonial. It is a time when the girls, who are of the age to

Denetsosie (at left) went to a Squaw Dance to meet the girl whom his father had selected for him. They liked each other.

marry, ask young men to dance. Some of the girls who dance make it known they want to get married. It also is the custom for the men to give the girls gifts of value after they have danced.

So Denetsosie went to the Squaw Dance. He met the woman. She was good looking. She was smart, too. He liked her, and she liked him. He stated, "She seemed to be a good woman and to have a good head on her shoulders."

But he returned to work. This was a time for thinking. His father continued to persuade him; and Denetsosie understood that he had to make the next move or lose this opportunity to get a wife. His father would come to see him every once in a while and tell him that the girl and her family wanted him to go over. But he kept putting it off. Finally, he went back to her place at harvest time.

It was sunset when he arrived. The girl was at the well getting water. They talked. She told him what had been happening. She showed him a hogan which had been built for them. She said, "That hogan over there was built for us, to be our home. But I was afraid you would not come."

He realized that he was to have a wife. And he knew that it was right. He was 22 years old; the girl was 20. The year was 1913.

The second time he went to see her she was drawing water at the well, and he learned that a hogan had been built for them.

They did not have a traditional Navajo ceremony. Denetsosie commented, "After three days a man named Hastiin Dilghoshii, who was a leader (naat'áanii) in Chinle, came and took us to that place."

The man took them to Éi'nishoodii Tsoh (Father Arnold) who gave them a marriage certificate. Then, Denetsosie recalled, "He gave us some counsel and instructed us in the ways of marriage. He said, 'There are many things to be desired in this world, and in the future you will come across some of these temptations and should prepare yourselves for them. When you have children take good care of them. Do not say bad things about each other. Do not mistreat each other. Hold on to each other as you should after being married today. Stay with each other until death parts you.' "

Denetsosie's new home, with his wife's family, was across the wash, at Taah yilk'id, east of the Valley Store, about four miles north of Chinle. The young husband had plenty of work to do. There were almost 700 sheep to care for. He supervised the shearing and the lambing, and he hauled wood.

The farm training by his stepfather was useful. He knew what to do when some of the ewes disowned their lambs after birth. He tied the ewes to posts and forced them to allow their offspring to suckle. He found foster mothers among the sheep and goats for lambs and kids whose mothers had died while giving birth or had dried up and could not give milk. It was very hard work for the whole family, especially for the young and strong Denetsosie who did more than his share.

He knew that raising a crop of lambs was something like raising a crop of corn. The lambs had to be given a chance to start growing, as did the tender young corn. The first care was very important. In addition, the horses had to be rounded up and brought in each morning.

The young husband loved and understood the sheep. It was hard work to care for them, but the lambs were healthy and his flocks prospered.

The men of the area helped him to dike the wash and to make ditches so that he could irrigate every time water came down the wash, which sometimes happened at night. He remembered how difficult it was to keep the laterals from washing out. The situation was just like when he was a boy — when the neighbors came to help his stepfather. They still helped each other.

Edward Stock, at that time superintendent of the Chinle sub-agency under John Collier, Commissioner of Indian Affairs, told the men they could fence their fields. Each landowner was given permission to cut one hundred posts from Tséłigainít'i' (White Rock Mesa). They went in a group to the mesa where they cut their quotas in two days. They hauled the posts out in wagons. Then they dug holes and set the posts. Wire was furnished by the sub-agency, with four or five strands being used. Denetsosie fenced his wife's land and also his own land at Wheatfields. He said that in those days he liked to work hard because it gave him a satisfying feeling. His life centered around two things — farming and taking care of sheep.

Some of the older men still planted in the old way. Denetsosie's father-in-law hated plows — said they ruined the land. If someone plowed a field for him he would be very upset and, as Denetsosie said, "he would fill the plowed ground back up and smooth it over." He used the old-time planting stick, and he raised good crops. Those who used the old method helped each other. Some made the holes. Others followed, dropping the seeds and pressing the dirt over them.

Some of the Navajos used the old-time planting stick, and they raised good crops of wheat, corn and other foods.

More Navajos began to farm at about that time, and many of them used plows, hoes and even picks to do the planting.

Corn became the main crop. The ears were gathered when they began to ripen, and they were stacked inside a fence. They were stirred and shifted occasionally until they were thoroughly dry. Then they were shucked and shelled. The kernels were put into a hole in the ground and covered with dirt for winter storage. In the spring the dirt was removed, and the corn was taken out for various uses.

The women prepared many kinds of food from the corn. There was naadą́ą́'bááh (cornbread), łee' shibéézh (corn roasted in ashes), tsá'ást'éí (paper-thin blue cornbread or piki made on a hot stone), and, of course, tóshchíín (cornmeal mush).

Women ground the corn on grinding stones and prepared many kinds of tasty and wholesome dishes from it.

Denetsosie recalled how the mush was made by placing a container made of clay in the coals of the campfire.

23

Water was poured immediately into the container. When the water was hot, the cornmeal was poured slowly into the water and stirred until it was a smooth, thick mass. A delicious flavor was obtained by mixing some of the ashes of a burned cedar branch with the water and meal. This was tóshchíín.

Sometimes the people made mush without the cedar. It was thicker and was called tanaashgiizh. Corn dumplings (k'íneeshbízhii) also were made. Nídínooyęshii (wide-spread bread) was something like pancakes. It was baked by pouring cornmeal batter onto ashes in an open pit. Naadą́ą́' náneeskaadí (round cornbread), with salt added, was baked on a flat hot rock. Another favorite food was cornmeal baked like a thick pudding.

Denetsosie said that ahwééh [or gohwééh] (coffee) was unknown on the Reservation in those days. Instead, the Navajos brewed drinks from hashk'aan ("wild bananas" or the green yucca fruit), dzidétso (peaches), various kinds of hosh bisgą' (cactus fruits), some weeds and gáagii bitł'ohchin (crow's onion).

When coffee did become known, the beans were a puzzle to the women who boiled them green and unroasted for hours. They could not understand why the water did not turn to a rich brown color with a pleasing aroma. When they discovered how to roast and grind the beans they began to make real coffee and to enjoy it. When they had no coffee, they roasted naadą́ą́' (corn) or tł'oh naadą́ą́' (wheat) as a substitute. Sugar was available at trading posts, as well as tea.

Nímasii yázhí (wild potatoes) often were found growing in the valleys, and long ago they had become a part of the Indians' meager diet. The Navajos learned, however, that the potatoes were edible only after they had been mixed with white clay. A dessert, also good when

Before coffee came into use on the Reservation, the Navajos brewed drinks from several kinds of plants, including the "wild bananas" (green fruit) of the yucca.

mixed with white clay, was chiił chin (sumac berries), sometimes called squaw berries.

People were closer in spirit to each other in those days than they are now, Denetsosie said. It was customary for people to visit each other, even though they lived far apart. They would stay two or three days. The various families lived in isolated areas and were eager to meet and talk with those from other parts of the Reservation.

If a Navajo family needed food, the members went to a neighbor's home and were fed. They were given flour, coffee and other food to take home. People were not stingy, even though they had little. Denetsosie regretted that this friendly custom was not followed so much during the last years of his life.

But to get back to Denetsosie, himself — he was happy and content with his wife. He often was away from home, singing at ceremonies, or just attending; but he always hurried home afterward. He did not want his wife to think that he was playing cards or running around with another woman. His wife never asked him what he did. He explained, "We had an understanding about these matters. She never bothered me about them. We thought well of each other."

Besides, he had much work to do, including such things as shoveling snow from the corrals during the winter, cutting tree branches and building shelters for the ewes at lambing time, hauling firewood and water, and taking care of the crops. In addition, the old ewes needed special feeding and attention; and the horses had to be cared for.

"You can't have many things in life if you lie around and sleep," he insisted. "You have to work, and work hard, for them. They won't just come to you. You cannot be lazy. You cannot expect to receive many things for doing nothing. You have to put out effort to receive something back."

He loved his fields and livestock. He understood that a person must offer love and kindness if his animals are to show the best possible growth and increase. He even had a ceremonial song which he sang to them, and they were raised without difficulty.

He also was very kind to his children. He never could say "No" to them. Once, he had a fine black lamb which he intended as a gift to his wife. But a child wanted it, and he gave it to the child. He stated, "When you have children, you earn things for their good. Even when they want lambs or horses you do not turn them down because it is for them that you work. It is much joy to have children and to see them grow in love and good health. If parents do not love their children and take good care of them, they lose them."

Truly, Denetsosie found great pleasure in the health and happiness of his wife and their four children.

However, there comes a time in the lives of all families when the children grow to be men and women. They develop other interests and move away. The father and mother grow older and become lonely. Home life, in the natural course of events, is broken.

And it was broken — suddenly and sadly — in Denetsosie's family. His wife died after they had been married about 18 years, and there was a period of mourning. Denetsosie took his children to Wheatfields, where they now live and are raising their own families. He had served on the grazing committee of the Navajo Tribal Council and had been able to obtain land for them. He says that people did not approve and that they talked about it — but that he ignored them. After the break-up of his family, he was very unhappy. He was alone, until one day at the Díwózhii bii'tó (upper Greasewood) Trading Post he met another woman whom he liked. They were married. The second wife was about 22 years old at the time. Denetsosie was about 44.

He left everything, including sheep and cattle, at his former home. He went to his new wife with nothing, and he lived with her at Kinłichíí' (Kinlichee, in the Red House area). The wife had the fields, but they had not been cultivated for several years. Early in the first spring they pitched a tent. They cleared the weeds and sagebrush. The wire had been removed from the fence posts, but he replaced it. He made the fields productive, and he and his new wife built a hogan and settled down to farm the land. They got about 40 sheep from his wife's mother,

Asdzą́ą́ Tódí'ch'íí'nii (Bitter Water Woman). The wife already owned them. She also had a trade slip for 10 dollars, and Denetsosie had one worth 55 dollars.

All of this happened more than 30 years before the original telling of this story by Denetsosie late in 1967.

STOCK REDUCTION

When the chapter system was established on the Navajo Reservation, beginning about 1928, the people in his area had wanted him to be an officer, but he was doubtful about it. He did not know what the duties and responsibilities would be. The people voted him in as chapter president, however, because they knew he was a good and capable man. He had no idea what a hard job it would be, but he did his best. And he served a total of 12 years as head of the Lukachukai Chapter.

He also was elected to the Navajo Tribal Council when it had only 12 members. He represented the Eleventh (Wheatfield) district, serving for four years. He was a good friend of Hastiin Adiits'a'ii (Henry Chee Dodge) and other Navajo leaders. He was becoming a man of some influence. He said, though, "At first I was in the dark. I did not know what I was getting into."

Because he was a member of the grazing committee, he became familiar with the problems of livestock owners.

Early in the 1930s those problems became more and more acute. The federal government had been watching the livestock situation on the Reservation for many years — 40, at least. Surveys had been made, but the purposes were not clear. Most of the Navajos knew little of what was going on. They felt that trouble was coming. The white man's government seemed to be doing things without letting the Navajos know the truth. And the situation made them angry.

It also made Denetsosie's work as a chapter president especially unpleasant, and he became really unpopular when the matter of livestock reduction finally was brought into the open by the late John Collier, then U. S. Commissioner of Indian Affairs.

As a chapter officer, Denetsosie attended many meetings at Tséghahoodzání (Window Rock), Naat'áanii Nééz (Shiprock), T'iists'óóznídeeshgiizh (Crownpoint), Shash bitoo (Fort Wingate) and other places. There was much discussion of the federal order to reduce all herds of domestic animals on the Reservation, from the smallest to the largest.

John G. Hunter of Fort Defiance, supervisor of the chapter officers, held a three-day conference at Lók'adeeshjin (Keams Canyon). On the third day, after long discussions and arguments, he told the officers there was nothing they could do about the situation. They were facing government regulations. All herd owners would have to reduce the numbers of their goats and sheep and other animals. Few would believe him when he told them that this move had been under consideration for 42 years.

Hunter explained that many of the people would blame them (the chapter officers) for everything.

"This will be like a mountain of water flooding down on you," he said.

According to Denetsosie, he was right.

The reduction program in Denetsosie's area, which started at the Díwózhii bii'tó (Greasewood) store, had just begun when trouble exploded. Women and children came running to the chapter officers, crying and shouting insults. They were faced with the loss of many prized sheep and goats.

The stock reduction program was a terrible blow, causing many tears and much bitterness. The Navajos loved their animals, and they needed them for food and other purposes. "You can't take my goats," cried one man, "unless you cut off my hands."

"You can't take my goats," stormed one angry man, "unless you cut my hands off while I'm still holding the goats."

Great emotion and bitterness was everywhere. There was much sorrow among the people, as well as among the chapter officers who had to carry out the orders. Women and children, and even some of the men, shed many tears.

The people always had been hard-pressed to earn a living and to feed their children, and now they were made desperate by this sad turn in their lives.

Denetsosie's own herd was reduced by 70 goats, six mules and some horses, donkies, sheep and cattle. He was forced to sell the cattle for a mere $12 a head. The horses, mules and donkies brought $3.50 each — the goats and sheep as little as a dollar. Some Navajos lost stock and received nothing in return.

Commissioner Collier told the Navajo people that, if they did not comply with the first reduction orders, they would be in an even worse condition. Failure to reduce their flocks would bring a stronger order in a short time. He told them that the program really was to protect the land (Mother Earth) from being worn out by over-grazing.

When World War II started, however, the situation faced by the United States helped to ease the tension of livestock reduction. The government had many more problems — very serious ones — to demand the attention of every department. And, by the end of the conflict, practically everything had been forgotten, except, of course, the sad and trying experiences through which the Navajo people again had passed.

Denetsosie had suffered great personal abuse throughout the enforcement of the reduction program and for some time afterward. Even his present wife, when he first asked her to marry him, had exclaimed, "You're not going to marry me. You took all of my livestock away."

In an interview (May, 1968) Denetsosie said, "It was not my fault for doing this to my people. I was a chapter president, and I had been on the tribal grazing committee. Jack Hunter and John Collier explained why the reduction had to be done, and they told me, and others, that we had to enforce it. They explained how sheep and goats eat the grasses right down to the roots and run around and tramp grasses and other plants until the plants die. They told us how goats and sheep make trails; then, when it rains, how the water starts running in these small ditches and makes them into big gullies."

He added, "I believed them. And I thought the reduction was for the good of my people. We had so much livestock that there was not feed enough for them, and the

31

quality of the animals was getting poorer and poorer. Still the Navajos in my chapter blamed me and other officers for taking away their sheep, goats, horses and other animals. They did not understand that we had been ordered by those above us to do it. Very few of them had attended meetings and heard what had been said. It really hurt us to enforce the reduction."

Many of his fellow Navajos in those years despised Denetsosie and other officers who aided in the reduction. They complained bitterly that Denetsosie and the others never felt sorry for the poor Navajos. They stopped using Denetsosie as a medicine man. For a time he was shut out by his own people.

But he did not become bitter. He was reviled, but he accepted the situation with serenity, feeling that he was doing the right thing. As the years went by, the ill feeling mellowed and was partially forgotten. Many Navajos came to understand the position that Denetsosie had been in. They began asking him again to serve as a medicine man, and he became a highly respected member of the Lukachukai community. He even served for a time as Tribal Judge for that area.

POLITICAL LIFE, HOPES FOR NAVAJOLAND

Denetsosie found time for a few years of comparative rest after the trying experiences of the stock reduction period and World War II. As mentioned above, he had been a member of the Navajo Tribal Council and its advisory committee, representing the Wheatfields district. The committee had discussed problems confronting the Navajos and ways and means of solving them to the best advantage and benefit of the people. Some of the research started at that time has continued to the present.

Subjects studied by the committee included schools, hospitals, paved roads, water wells and dams and water masters, land management and supervisors, and construction of a sawmill.

For example, to learn how much moisture was needed in the Lukachukai area for crops, a ditch boss was hired to study the water supply, and Denetsosie was named to the job for a four-year term.

He commented later, "As with all of the work that I did for my people, when a decision was made that the people in my area did not like they blamed me."

Another important matter before the people concerned natural resources. Many kinds of minerals had been found on Reservation lands. Gold, silver, copper and uranium were known to exist in quantities that would justify producing for commercial purposes. Asphalt rock, building stone, clays, gypsum and lime were available in great commercial quantities. Coal was plentiful in two areas of the Reservation — Black Mesa, Arizona, and the Gallup-Durango region in New Mexico and Colorado.

An additional problem involved the fact that white people began to arrive on the Reservation without permission. They were making certain tests regarding resources, and there were no established rules at that time to prevent their coming and making those tests. Denetsosie declared, "They used to say that they wanted to help the Navajos, but they really wanted the profits from the oil wells and the turquoise, silver, coal and other mines."

This situation later was corrected and strict rules were made governing such activities. In recent years he felt that the mineral resources of the Navajo country were being properly protected for the use and benefit of present and future generations of his people.

As a member of the grazing committee, he had found that one of the most important problems was the providing of water for livestock and domestic use by drilling

White men began to exploit the Reservation's natural resources, such as oil and gas, which belonged to the Navajos.

wells. He recalled that the first drilling site was on the west side of the Kennedy Store, near present-day Lukachukai. Another site was across the canyon on the north side. A third was close to the Tséyi' Ch'ínlį́ (Canyon de Chelly) area. The main consideration for locating a drilling site was the number of families living nearby who would be benefited.

Operation of the flour mill at Bis dootłizh deez'á (Round Rock) had to be abandoned because little water was available. It would have served the Wheatfields and Lukachukai areas. Denetsosie said that the people wanted the mill badly and talked about it a lot. Many meetings were held, especially in Shiprock. The mill was built and it was tried for a couple of summers. He explained, "At first there was enough water to run the mill, but there ceased to be enough and so the mill was stopped."

In spite of his many activities and responsibilities, Denetsosie, as a former councilman and a respected member of the tribe, found time to speak to groups of children on numerous occasions because he was a firm believer in the value of an education. He usually advised them on such matters as getting an education and living good and worthwhile lives. He knew that the children of today are different from the children of his boyhood days in their outlook and in regard to the future facing them. He felt that the old days were good days, and he liked to remind the young people of them; but he also understood the needs of the Navajos at present and in the future. He said:

"I feel that education offers the greatest hope for those who live on the Reservation. I urge you children to continue your education. When you make good, you will realize how important it was. Some day certain of you will be leaders of your people. One of the things the Navajo people want most is for their children to go to school and apply themselves to study. They do not want the young people to waste their time.

"Getting an education is like learning to be a medicine man. You have to go and take part, even in cold weather or during the night, in order to learn all the different things there are to be learned.

"I want the children of today to think about their future. I want them to remember what their grandparents say to them. The old days have passed away, and the new and modern ways are here, but youngsters should take the advice and counsel of those who have gone before."

Regarding marriage, Denetsosie said:

"From a long time back the father of a boy would go to the parents of a girl and talk about the marriage of his son and their daughter. First, he would ask about their clans because he did not want his son to marry someone who might be related to him, even distantly.

"The girl's parents would wish to know what kind of a boy wanted to marry their girl. They would ask about clans, too.

"If the young people were old enough for marriage, and not related, the boy's parents would pay something for the girl. The offer might be twelve horses, belts, bracelets or anything else of value.

"Meanwhile, the father would talk to the son. He would advise him to herd sheep, bring water, plant crops and take care of things around his mother-in-law's place. He would tell him to take good care of the girl, and not to live in the same hogan with the mother-in-law, but, rather, to stay with the girl in another dwelling."

Then he added:

"When the woman begins to have children, the father should work for them and help feed them. Even birds bring food to their babies from sunup to sundown."

Denetsosie remembered vividly one particular wedding ceremony at Bee'ak'e halchíí' (Red Lake) — a white man taking a Navajo girl as his bride.

The girl's father had told all the relatives that he was going to have a white son-in-law, and they all came when it was time for the wedding.

The girl brought in the basket of corn mush and set it in front of the man she was to marry. Her father sat by the basket and blessed the mush from east, south, west and north. He told the man to take some of the mush with two fingers from each of those directions. The girl did the same thing. After that had been done, the people talked to the young couple about how they should live

36

At the wedding of a Navajo girl and a white man, the girl's father blessed the corn mush from east, south, west and north.

as married people in the future. They pointed out that the wife should take care of her husband; she should keep her house clean; the in-laws should not gossip about them, and the mother-in-law should love them.

Denetsosie also commented about the fact that today many Navajos are married to members of other tribes and races. He had an in-law who is of another Indian tribe. He said, "Such in-laws are common. We are not going to send these people away. We must think highly of each other and not use harsh words. We must fit into this modern world and take our rightful place in it."

He liked to discuss another matter, too. That is the role the medicine man plays in the life of a Navajo. He said that when someone is sick, the ill person always needs the help of the medicine man. The medicine man must follow a wedding with a Navajo sing, too.

He added that it was the custom in the old days that there be a special sing before a son-in-law could look at his mother-in-law. This is not necessary these days, though, he explained. The people do as they please.

The old people used to say that if there wasn't a sing for seeing the mother-in-law, and if the son-in-law happened to meet her accidentally, something would happen to his eyes. Denetsosie said that he had known cases where the son-in-law looked at the mother-in-law without the benefit of a sing, but that nothing ever happened to the son-in-law.

TRADING POSTS, RODEOS AND FAIRS

Denetsosie believed that some significant factors that brought rapid changes to the Reservation over the years were the trading posts, on-reservation schools (a classroom of not more than 30 children for each teacher — Treaty of 1868), missions, rodeos and fairs.

He insisted that most of the traders were good friends of the Navajos when he was a young man. The traders at that time were generous with the people. They were liberal in allowing credit, too. He explained that he never had seen a trader shake his head "No." He added, "Nowadays a trader sometimes asks questions and tells you that you owe so much on a bill and that you must pay."

He never had heard a trader tell a customer he was lying about his needs, nor had he heard a trader question a Navajo's ability to pay his debts. Usually the trader knew the women of each household and could depend on them to bring in fine rugs to take care of a debt. And he was fair to the women in his dealing.

"In those days business was different," Denetsosie said; and he explained how a trade or bargain was made:

After the trader and the Navajo woman finally came to an agreement about the price of a rug, the trader would give treats to her family, usually canned tomatoes and crackers.

"A certain ritual was involved in the sale of a rug. The woman brought the rug into the trading post and spread it out on a table. The trader felt it and walked around it, inspecting it closely for flaws. He also noted the good qualities. Then he made an offer. If the weaver and her family accepted, the sale was concluded. If they asked for a higher price, there was another period of discussion and argument. This might go on all day, maybe longer.

"When the final agreement was reached, the trader would bring out canned tomatoes and crackers, and the weaver and her family would eat before selecting the items she wanted.

"Just to be friendly, the trader often would give the man his choice of cloth for a shirt, or he would give the woman material for a blouse, including cloth for the lining. In those days the trader and his Navajo customers were friendly and respected each other."

Traders usually had a hogan right next to the store. This was for the use of the Navajos who had come a long way and who wished to stay overnight. Often the trader would say, "Take some of my firewood and have a warm place to sleep." Then he gave the visitors flour, bacon and coffee — and the use of pots and pans. In the summer the trader always had a pail of water and a cup, and, year 'round, tobacco and matches.

At Christmas time the trader gave a party for his Navajo people. It was the custom, and the people looked forward to it. They would come from miles around. It was a great feast for them. The women hurried to finish their rugs, so that they could take them to the post at that time. The spirit of Christmas was with the trader, and he paid more for the rugs then. The children were excited as they thought of the candy, fruit and little toys they would receive. Denetsosie believed that the traders have meant much in the lives of Navajo people but that, today, "too many of them are here just to get our money."

Regarding schools, he said that he has advocated more and better schools for the Reservation ever since he was a young man. Specifically, he helped promote the Bureau of Indian Affairs schools at Many Farms and Lukachukai. He said:

"I always have wanted schools for our children. And, although we have many of them now, I think there should be more. I am sure that good education is the most important thing for the Navajos." And he added, "I really like the things that the people are doing at the Rough Rock Demonstration School. In teaching both the Navajo way and the white man's way they are fitting our children for life in both worlds."

During Denetsosie's younger years, most traders had Christmas parties for the Navajos in their areas, with plenty of food for all and special candy, fruit and toys for the children.

He thought that the missions have done much good, too; and he had a really high regard for the missionaries. He felt that they generally "help us when we have some problems that we can't straighten out among ourselves." But he added that some Navajos "follow the Christians around just because they can get used clothing and other articles." This he did not like.

Denetsosie also felt that rodeos have contributed greatly to the changing world of the Navajos. He said that these events have been an important factor in bringing the people together in a social way, just as ceremonies, weddings and get-togethers at the chapter houses have done. More and more there is evidence of the Navajos accepting the modern way of life. Their dress and modes of entertainment show this. And they seem to enjoy the change.

Denetsosie believed that rodeos have been good for the Navajos, and he remembered vividly some of the early events for which he had been a strong booster, especially the one at Round Rock.

He believed that rodeos have been an education to most of the Navajos. He recalled that Frank Harvey, Bucker Barney and several other men who were young at the time were responsible for the rodeo at Lukachukai. In 1935 they got together to organize the events to enliven the dead days of summer. They began to practice riding wild cattle and bucking horses, and the time came when they staged their rodeo at Round Rock. They also promoted such an event at the Window Rock Fair Grounds, where it now is held annually.

The spectacles feature all the events of big-time rodeos — including saddle bronc riding, bareback riding, trick roping and riding, boys' calf riding, steer wrestling, calf roping and even Brahma bull riding. The Navajo rodeo

Denetsosie credited the fairs, also, with being big helps in the progress of the Navajos. The people attend in a holiday spirit, all dressed in their best — many in the deeply-loved old-time costumes.

clowns have caught on and are a delight, especially for the children. It has proved to be a good way to get the people together; and they like it.

As a member of various rodeo committees, Denetsosie always was an avid booster of the events.

He also gave much credit to the annual fairs for the recent development of the Navajos. The fairs at Window Rock and Shiprock prompt the people to dress in their best and to make real holidays of the affairs, he said.

They like to dress up. The older ladies often still wear the old-time costumes of rich-colored velvet blouses and full skirts of bright contrasting colors, as well as good buckskin shoes. They wear fine bracelets and silver necklaces adorned with turquoise. Colorful blankets make their costumes complete. The men also dress in their best, with their turquoise and silver jewelry, their fancy belts, fine shirts and good trousers.

The cowboys of the rodeo are especially discriminating about their "gear." They usually have new broadbrimmed hats, rolled sharply at the sides, bright western-style shirts, good riding pants and perhaps chaps of leather or angora. They are just as particular about their horses, for which they have fancy saddles and bridles decorated with silver ornaments on the nose-pieces and rosettes down the cheek straps.

Denetsosie noted that Navajo young people and children are now so "Americanized" that they blend with the well-dressed Anglo boys and girls. Often they leave their parents to watch the parade or rodeo with their white friends. There is no segregation in the modern generation on the Navajo Reservation.

The Navajo-American young people also participate in the white man's dances. They travel in fast cars. They think nothing of driving to Gallup, Window Rock, Shiprock, Flagstaff, Farmington and other places to see a rodeo or to attend a dance. They meet other boys and girls of their own and other tribes, as well as white boys and girls. It all leads to a better understanding.

Denetsosie, like other older Navajos, wondered what is happening to their culture and customs. Most of them, he said, hope sincerely that the younger generation will adapt itself to both the Navajo and the Anglo ways of life and thus assure its own — and future generations — of taking a proper and worthwhile place in American society and in the future of our great country.

The Rough Rock Demonstration School (DINÉ, Inc. — Demonstration in Navajo Education) is aware of what is happening, and it is making a great and successful effort to preserve

Navajo culture and life. At the same time, it is preparing the children, through proper education, to contribute in a meaningful manner to their own people as well as to America and the world.

All of which made Denetsosie happy.

Denetsosie died of a heart attack on April 7, 1969, at his home a few miles northwest of the center of the Lukachukai community. Although his health had been failing for more than two years, with periods of hospitalization, he had kept a keen interest in the affairs of the local school, the community and the tribe. He also had been active as a member of the Board of Directors of the Navajo Culture Center which functions out of Fort Defiance. In addition, because of the esteem in which he was held as a leader and as a medicine man, he had conducted some five-night sings, as well as smaller ceremonies.

His wife, 57 years of age, continues to live at their home near the highway which runs from Mexican Water through Rock Point, past Round Rock and Lukachukai to Wheatfields and Window Rock.

As this story of Denetsosie's life was being published, all of his children were doing well. The four offspring by his first wife were farming in the Wheatfields area. Of the three by his second wife, a son had been graduated from high school and was living near Lukachukai; a daughter had attended college for three years and was working at Tsé nitsaa deez'á (Rock Point), and another daughter was in the eighth grade at Many Farms at the time Denetsosie was being interviewed. A stepdaughter by his present wife also was working at Rock Point.

Denetsosie made it clear that he wanted all of his grandchildren to be educated.

He concluded, "My grandfather used to talk to me about respect toward all people. So, these days I still am like that. I never get mad or say any bad things to any people or about people. I respect all of them — Navajos, other Indians and white men."

This philosophy — this serenity of spirit — pervaded Denetsosie's life for many decades. It helped to explain the high regard in which he was held.

He stood tall as a man who knew and respected both the Navajo culture and the Anglo way of life.

ACKNOWLEDGMENTS

Many thanks to Allen Harvey, Lewis Singer, Laura Wallace and Jim Claw who have contributed their expertise in Navajo to this book.

Indian Education at Rough Rock . . .

*T*HE NAVAJO MEMBERS who comprise the Board of Education of the Rough Rock Demonstration School are highly educated men in Navajo culture and language, and they have organized the curriculum at Rough Rock to include both of these elements in addition to the basic curriculum offered in good elementary schools across the nation.

Through its action the Board at Rough Rock has pioneered in correcting the omission of Indian culture which has plagued Indian education for too many years. Clyde Kluckhohn, in his excellent book *Mirror for Man,* goes to the heart of matters when he points out that just as the person who has lost his memory no longer is normal so the society cut off from its past is inconceivable. Any culture provides the individual in it with designs for acting, feeling and believing. Put simply, it is a man's culture which humanizes him beyond the animal level.

Seen in this perspective, the so-called "Indian Education" of the past which omitted and even repressed things Indian was an insidious dehumanizing process, however well-meaning some parts of it may have been.

Fully aware of man's need to know his own people and their beliefs, Rough Rock's Board changed the inconceivable pattern of past Indian education. In so doing the members have restored balance and, thus, harmony to the world that nurtures their children. The talent for doing this always has been central to Navajo religion. It comes as no surprise that they have had the wisdom to apply the same restorative principles to shaping the education of their children.

The Navajo Curriculum Center is proud to offer this book as one segment of the great journey to understanding which the Board has charted for the community, its children and people everywhere who are interested in themselves and others — who, out of this interest, act to advance our knowledge of, and appreciation for, the human condition in all of its great variety.

Martin Hoffman, Director
Navajo Curriculum Center

Dillon Platero, Director
Rough Rock Demonstration School